FIRENZE
MVSEI

# Accademia Gallery

## Franca Falletti
Director of the Accademia Gallery

D1016113

GIUNTI

*Graphic design*: Franco Bulletti
*Cover design*: Laura Belforte *and* Fabio Filippi

*Editorial manager*: Claudio Pescio
*Editing*: Augusta Tosone

*Translation*: Ailsa Wood for Lexis, Florence

*Photographic credits*:Giunti Archive / Foto Rabatti-Domingie, Florence

Published by Giunti Gruppo Editoriale, Florence
Third edition: July 1999
ISBN 88-09-2174-X

# CONTENTS

The Accademia Gallery 7

The Gallery of the *Slaves* and the Tribuna of *David* 13

Florentine Rooms 26

Hall of the Colossus 35

Side wings of the Tribuna 43

Nineteenth Century Room 46

Byzantine Rooms 48

First floor Rooms 61

*Index* 78

**MICHELANGELO BUONARROTI,** *David* (detail)

*ENOUGH BOOKS have been written about the public museums in Florence run by the Fine Arts and Historic Works Commission to fill a large library. This is hardly surprising when one considers that the artistic heritage preserved in our museums has been famous throughout the world for centuries. For hundreds of years writers, scholars and travellers of every nationality and country have been attempting to describe all that the Florentine museums contain. They have made great efforts to explain why these museums are so fascinating, and to lead a path through paintings and sculptures for both the uninformed but willing visitor and the refined and jaded intellectual.*

*Over time, however, the museums have altered their aspect and their layout, the exhibitions have been arranged in new ways, the collections have been enriched (or impoverished). Attributions of works in the museums have also changed, restorations have transformed the appearance of many pieces, the rise and fall of aesthetic tendencies have led to reorganisation and the exhibition of differing works. All these things are constantly taking place within the public collections because museology and the history of art, like any intellectual endeavour, are in a constant state of progress and transformation. This explains why the literature surrounding the Florentine museums (like that of any of the world's great art collections) is so immense, and in a process of continual updating and change.*

*The perfect, definitive guide to a museum, any museum, does not and cannot exist.*

*The premise seems obvious, but is nonetheless necessary in order to understand the point of the publication introduced by these lines. From the moment when, in accordance with the application of the Ronchey law 4/93, the Giunti publishing house group took over the running of the support services within the Florentine museum system, it was decided to start at once on a standardised series of illustrated guides. These guides, displaying the cuneiform flower of "Firenze Musei" on the cover, guarantee that at the year of publication the state of each museum is exactly that described in the guide.*

*Certain things are obviously necessary if a museum guide is to aspire to reliability, official standing and at the same time enjoy a wide distribution: accuracy of information, high quality reproductions, an easily manageable format, a reasonable cost and – not least – a clearly written text (without, naturally, being banal or lacking in precision). Readers will judge for themselves if the guide which follows this introduction reaches these standards. I have no doubt that this will be a serious and committed judgement, just as myself and the Publisher of this guide have been serious and committed in attempting to meet the cultural needs of whoever visits our museums in the best way and with every possible care.*

*Head of the Fine Arts
and Historic Works Commission
of Florence, Pistoia and Prato
(Antonio Paolucci)*

**Lorenzo Monaco**, *Christ as the Man of Sorrows*

# The Accademia Gallery

The Accademia Gallery is one of the best known museums in the world today, and during the fourteen hours it is open on an average day, it is visited by up to six thousand tourists, making a total of almost a million visitors per year.

The Gallery is situated on the former site of a monastery, San Matteo, and a convent, San Niccolò di Cafaggio, which occupied the whole block between piazza Santissima Annunziata and via Ricasoli.

Its collection consists of works of art from the Accademia del Disegno (academy of drawing), founded by Cosimo I de' Medici in 1563, and from the Accademia di Belle Arti (academy of fine arts), an art school founded by Grand Duke Pietro Leopoldo of Lorraine in 1784. The aim of this collection of works was thus originally didactic, and useful to young artists who could study and copy the great examples of the past.

The abolition of monasteries and ecclesiastical brotherhoods in 1785 and 1808 brought numerous religious paintings to the rooms of the recently founded school, and many of these are still part of the Gallery's vast collection of paintings today.

Then in 1873, Michelangelo's *David*, previously situated in Piazza della Signoria in front of Palazzo Vecchio, was also transferred to the Accademia, which subsequently began to be known throughout the world as the Michelangelo Museum. In 1909 it was joined by the *Slaves* and *Saint Matthew*, and in 1939, the *Pietà from Palestrina*.

In the meantime, the collection of paintings was continually diminishing: Beato Angelico's pictures were transferred to the San Marco museum where they are still displayed today, and many masterpieces were moved to the Uffizi Gallery.

Since 1980 the Gallery has been considerably enlarged. A collection of plaster casts by the 19th century sculptors Lorenzo Bartolini and Luigi Pampaloni has been set up in the huge room on the ground floor, known as the "room of the Tuscans". The highly prized collection of late Gothic Florentine paintings has been situated on the first floor, in four rooms which were not previously used for permanent exhibitions, along with the unique group of Russian icons from the private collections of the Grand Dukes of Lorraine.

**MICHELANGELO BUONARROTI (?)**, *Pietà from Palestrina*

## MICHELANGELO'S SCULPTURES

The *David* was the first of Michelangelo's sculptures to be displayed in the Accademia Gallery. It was brought here in 1873, allegedly for conservation reasons; but although quite serious damage was undoubtedly caused by the long centuries passed under the elements and bad restoration works, many other factors were involved in the decision to remove the masterpiece from its original location in Piazza della Signoria. The intention was actually to hold a large exhibition dedicated to Michelangelo to celebrate the fourth centenary of his birth, in 1875, and subsequently set up a real Michelangelo Museum with original works, plaster casts and drawings. This duly took place: around the period of the First World War the museum displayed, alongside the works we can still admire today, the *Fiume Torso*, now in Casa Buonarroti and the *Victory* group, now in the Bargello museum. There were also numerous plaster casts of the great artist's works, which were preserved in other Italian and foreign collections.

Lastly, in 1939, the *Pietà* discovered in the Barberini chapel in Palestrina, near Rome, was brought here; Michelangelo's authorship of this work is however denied today by the most authoritative experts.

## THE NINETEENTH CENTURY ROOM

In 1985, works by teachers from the 19th century Accademia were displayed in the pleasant space which used to be the passageway for women from the San Matteo hospital. The collection of plaster casts, in particular, has found its permanent home here, which was donated to the Italian State by the heirs of the sculptor Lorenzo Bartolini after his death in 1850. Alongside these are casts by another great 19th century Tuscan sculptor, Luigi Pampaloni, and some paintings closely linked to the history of the Accademia; these were painted by pupils who later became famous artists (like Silvestro Lega or Cesare Mussini) when they were admitted to the Accademia or when they completed their studies.

The plaster casts displayed are nearly all models made by the artist and not, as one might think, casts of finished works. They should therefore be considered more autographical than the final marble versions, as they were made by the artist in person. Bartolini in particular had a highly organised studio, which often continued his work while he was away. In order for the finished work to be the same as the model, dark dots had to be followed, which can still be seen on many casts and are actually iron nails inserted while the plaster was still wet.

The large number of busts here are proof of the popularity of the portraiture genre with the 19th century European bourgeoisie, prior to the advent of photography.

THE COLLECTION OF GOLD-BACKGROUND PANELS

The Accademia Gallery's unique collection of panels painted on gold background is located on the ground floor, in the so-called Byzantine rooms, and the four rooms on the first floor. Various subsequent additions have enlarged the collection, which was recently rearranged, in accordance with the latest critical studies of the subject, to allow these Florentine works of art from the period between Giotto and Masaccio to be seen clearly and completely. The three ground floor rooms house the works of late 13th century painters, the contemporaries of Giotto, Taddeo Gaddi and Bernardo Daddi, and the Orcagna family, leading figures in Florence after the great plague of 1348. On the first floor are works by both lesser artists and great masters, which exemplify the various trends of late Gothic painting in the Tuscan capital. The greatest of these are the intense *Pietà* painted by Giovanni da Milano and the shining panels by Lorenzo Monaco, each phase of whose work is recorded here.

All the works are from religious buildings in Florence and the rest of Tuscany and some polyptychs are still complete with cusps, pinnacles, newels and spiral side posts, and predellas, providing us with an opportunity to understand the complexity and perfection such items required from carpenters and carvers.

View of the Byzantine Rooms

THE COLLECTION OF MUSICAL INSTRUMENTS

Four large rooms in the adjoining Luigi Cherubini State School of Music are currently being prepared to accommodate the historical collection of musical instruments from the School.

The collection will include items unique in the world, like the so-called *viola medicea*, made in 1690 by Antonio Stradivari to the commission of Prince Ferdinando de' Medici, or the psaltery made in three types of marble, decorated with the Medici coat of arms and a rhyming dedication. The most important group in the exhibition comes from the collection of the Grand Dukes, first the Medici and later the Lorraines, and was brought from the Palazzo Pitti in 1863 and 1926.

The museum of musical instruments will be linked to the Accademia Gallery within a year and will become a part of its display route, in keeping with the spirit of historical conservation which has also been the basis for other important preparatory additions in recent years, like the 19th century room. The Music School was originally part of the Accademia di Belle Arti, and was the second class after that which included painting, sculpture and architecture, and before applied arts.

*Marble psaltery* from the Medici's collection

11

Tribuna of *David*

# THE GALLERY OF THE SLAVES AND THE TRIBUNA OF DAVID

*This large room is shaped like a Latin cross-shaped church at the centre of which, underneath the circular skylight, stands the* David. *The side wings and Gallery of the* Slaves *occupy the space of the medieval San Matteo hospital, while the Tribuna was especially built to the design of the architect Emilio de Fabris between 1873 and 1882. This new construction was the subject of many heated disputes, partly because it seemed too narrow for Michelangelo's majestic statue and the background too fragmented by the relief mouldings. Despite these reservations, which to an extent we share today, the room is particularly charming and is one of the most intensely exciting museum areas in the whole world.*

*Standing at the end of the Gallery of the* Slaves *and looking towards the* David *it is easy to understand why almost a million tourists visit these rooms every year and why many of them experience a perception of beauty which is strong and sudden enough to almost overwhelm the senses.*

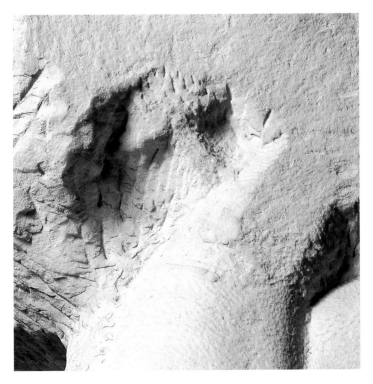

MICHELANGELO BUONARROTI, *Slaves: Atlas* (detail)

**MICHELANGELO
BUONARROTI**
*Slaves*

c. 1530

Marble
Height 256, 267, 263, 277
Sculptures inv.
no. 1078, 1079, 1080, 1081

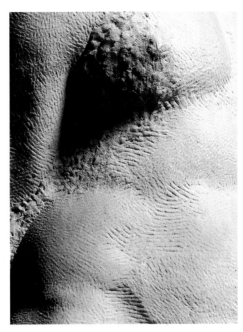

The four sculptures were intended to decorate the base of a complicated mausoleum to be raised under the dome of St. Peter's in the Vatican, for the remains of Pope Julius II della Rovere. The design had a rather tormented history and after undergoing radical modifications to reduce the size, the mausoleum was placed in S. Pietro in Vincoli where it remains to this day. The unfinished *Slaves* were donated after Michelangelo's death to Cosimo I de' Medici and placed by him in the Buontalenti grotto in Boboli whence they were transferred to the Accademia in 1909.

The *Slaves* are a useful introduction to an understanding of Michelangelo's unfinished work: their imperfect forms manage to convey a universal meaning to the sensation of an inhuman struggle to free themselves from the marble, which is evident to everyone who sees them.

*Slaves:*
*The Young Slave*
(whole on the left
and detail above)

c. 1530

Marble
Height 256
Sculptures inv. no. 1080

The first of the four *Slaves* displayed along the walls of the gallery leading to the Tribuna of *David* is known as *The Young Slave*. He is depicted with slightly bent knees, as if burdened by a weary step, and his left arm is folded across his face, while his right arm slips behind his hip. Emerging from a block of marble which, at the back, seems still untouched, the different parts of the figure itself have been finished to various degrees: the head is roughly outlined, the left side of the torso more finished than the right. However on each part of the surface the marks of the tools used by Michelangelo in his long creative process are still visible.

**MICHELANGELO BUONARROTI**
*Slaves:*
*The Bearded Slave*
(detail on the left)

c. 1530

Marble
Height 263
Sculptures inv. no. 1081

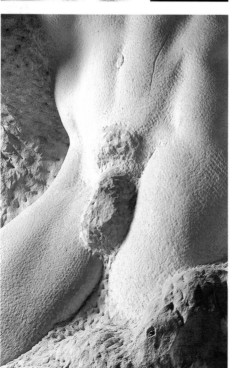

*Slaves:*
*The Awakening Slave*
(whole on the right
and detail on the left)

c. 1530

Marble
Height 267
Sculptures inv. no. 1078

The powerful limbs of this virile figure struggle to emerge from one side of the imposing block of marble.
The roughly outlined features of the face can barely be made out, and the right leg, bent over the left, protrudes forward to mirror the movement of the right arm. The result is a tense and dynamic composition which fully expresses the struggle of the material to break out of its own limits.

MICHELANGELO
BUONARROTI
*Slaves:*
*The Bearded Slave*
(on the left)

c. 1530
Marble
Height 263
Sculptures inv. no. 1081

*The Bearded Slave* is the most nearly finished of the four *Slaves*. The face is covered by a thick, curly beard and the thighs are encircled by a strip of cloth. The fine modelling of the torso, the surface finished with soft sensitivity to light and clear evidence of relief modelling, reveals a careful and profound study of anatomy.

*Slaves: Atlas*
(on the right)

c. 1530
Marble
Height 277
Sculptures inv. no. 1079

This *Slave* is known as *Atlas* because he seems to be carrying a huge weight on his head; however the weight is in fact the head itself, which is not separate and cannot be distinguished. The legs seem to be parted and the bent arms struggle to support the massive weight bearing down on the wide shoulders.

**MICHELANGELO**
**BUONARROTI**
*Saint Matthew*

1505-1506
Marble
Height 271
Sculptures inv. no. 1077

The *Saint Matthew* was originally to be part of a series of the twelve apostles, a commission given to Michelangelo in 1503 for the columns of Florence cathedral. In the event the sculptor only worked on one, which is also unfinished, for which reason it was left abandoned in the Cathedral Vestry courtyard until 1831.

It was moved to the Accademia di Belle Arti where it was first placed in a niche in the courtyard and later, in 1909, in the Gallery near the *Slaves*.

**MICHELANGELO**
**BUONARROTI**
*David*

1501-1504
Marble
Height 517
Sculptures inv. no. 1076

The *David* was originally commissioned by the Florence Cathedral Vestry Board to be placed as a decoration in the Cathedral. It was sculpted by Michelangelo between 1501 and 1504, when it was placed in front of the Palazzo Vecchio, following much discussion and debate among the main contemporary Florentine artists.

**MICHELANGELO BUONARROTI**
*David*
(whole and details
on following pages)

The Giant, as it became known, became a symbol of the civil freedom and virtue of republican Florence, and it remained in its original location until 1873 when it was transferred, using a complex support structure resting on wheels, inside the Accademia di Belle Arti, where it can still be admired today.

The sculpture portrays the future king of Israel in a similar form and pose to a triumphant hero of classical Greece. This clearly distances Michelangelo's *David* from those previously made by Donatello and Verrocchio which, adhering more closely to the biblical text, depicted David as a slender boy, unaware of his divine mission.

The statue's perfect modelling, the calm and determined strength of the expression and its imposing size have made it one of the best-known and most admired works of art in the world.

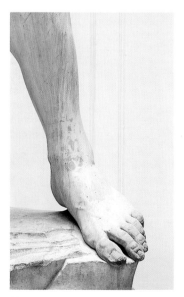
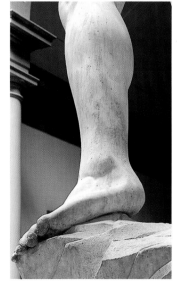

# FLORENTINE ROOMS

*These three rooms are dedicated to 15th century paintings. While some masterpieces are displayed here, like the canvas showing* Scenes of Hermit Life *by Paolo Uccello and the* Virgin and Child with the Young St. John and Two Angels *by Botticelli, the everyday production of the most active studios in Renaissance Florence is also represented. Among these were Ghirlandaio's and Cosimo Rosselli's, where the great masters worked in close contact with assistants and errand boys on the numerous paintings which were to decorate the thousands of altars of the city's churches, large and small.*

**ANDREA
DI GIUSTO MANZINI**
*Madonna of the Girdle*

1437
Tempera on wood
185×220
Inv. 1890 no. 3236

This painting, which is signed "Andrea de Florentia", comes from the church of Santa Margherita a Cortona (Arezzo), and is the work of a Florentine painter active during the first half of the 15th century. The artist is clearly familiar with the examples of his peers, other painters such as Paolo Uccello and Fra Angelico, but solidly linked to the Gothic tradition, as this altarpiece shows in its use of gold-leaf background and the division of the space into three, which recalls the 14th century polyptychs.

**PAOLO UCCELLO**
*Scenes of Hermit Life*
(and detail below)

c. 1460

Oil on canvas
81×111
Inv. 1890 no. 5381

The subject of this painting by Paolo Uccello is not easily interpreted but is certainly linked to a path of meditation and spiritual improvement through prayer. The following episodes can be identified: *The Stigmata of Saint Francis, Saint Jerome worships the Crucifix, The Appearance of the Virgin to Saint Bernard* and *Saint Benedict preaches to His Brethren.*

**LO SCHEGGIA**
*"Cassone Adimari"*
(whole and details)

c. 1450

Tempera on wood
63×280
Inv. 1890 no. 8457

This was originally listed as *"Cassone Adimari"* because it was thought to be the front panel of a wedding chest belonging to the Adimari family. The painting was later recognised as part of a *spalliera*, a wall decoration, and was attributed to Giovanni di Ser Giovanni, known as Lo Scheggia, the brother of Masaccio. The images depicted here concern a wedding feast and portray the streets, monuments (the Baptistry can be seen on the left), landscapes and customs of Renaissance Florence with vivacity and extraordinary wealth of detail.

**COSIMO ROSSELLI**
*Saint Barbara*

1468
Tempera on wood
215×219
Inv. 1890 no. 8635

Cosimo Rosselli, head of a well-equipped, active family-run studio, painted this gorgeous panel for the chapel of Saint Barbara and Saint Quiricus in the basilica of the Santissima Annunziata in Florence. This chapel belonged to the so-called "Teutonic nation", i.e. to the Germans and Flemings. Saint Barbara was the patron saint of artillery and therefore she is holding up the tower as a symbol of a line of fortification and crushing a conquered warrior beneath her feet. The composition of the painting recalls details from works by other contemporary Florentine artists, like Pollaiuolo's panel for the Portuguese cardinal's chapel in San Miniato and Ghirlandaio's fresco in the church of Sant'Andrea in Cercina, but it is painted with skill and dignity.

**NERI DI BICCI**
*Annunciation*

1464
Tempera on wood
286×178
Inv. 1890 no. 8622

This panel comes from the church of Santa Maria del Sepolcro, known as "delle Campora", for which it was commissioned in 1464 by Agnolo Vettori, an outstanding figure in 15th century Florentine politics, several times prior and gonfalonier of the Republic in 1458. Heir to an ancient Florentine studio, founded by his grandfather Lorenzo di Bicci and continued by his father, Bicci di Lorenzo, Neri di Bicci often reproduced traditional compositions over the years with his impeccable technique, making only the slightest modifications. Worthy of note in this *Annunciation* (one of many painted by this artist) is the detail of the small board at the bottom showing the Crucifixion, and the complex architecture of the background.

**DOMENICO GHIRLANDAIO**
*Saint Stephen between Saints James and Peter*

1493
Oil on wood
175×174
Inv. 1890 no. 16221

In the past this panel was attributed to Sebastiano Mainardi, a pupil of Ghirlandaio, but it was recently recognised as work of the master himself. A few years after it was painted, perhaps in 1513, the figure of Saint Stephen was repainted to look like Saint Jerome, by the hand of Fra' Bartolomeo, according to traditional accounts. 19th century restoration work then cancelled this modification. In this composition the touch of Ghirlandaio, noted for his lively narrative and decorative elements, is conspicuous in the unusual majesty of the three sculptural figures which strikingly emerge from the chiaroscuro effect of the niches.

**SANDRO BOTTICELLI**
*Virgin with Child*
*with the Young Saint*
*John and Two Angels*

c. 1468
Tempera on wood
85×64
Inv. 1890 no. 3166

This work is from Botticelli's early phase; the pleasant composition clearly shows the stylistic characteristics of Filippo Lippi, in whose studio Sandro was still training.

This composition with its diffuse structure was to be very successful in subsequent years and was repeated in numerous plaster or terracotta bas-reliefs for private devotional use.

**SANDRO BOTTICELLI (?)**
*Virgin of the Sea*

c. 1475-1480
Tempera on wood
40×28
Inv. 1890 no. 8456

This small panel, which owes its name to the dim seascape in the background, has always been one of the most admired works by visitors to the Gallery. However the critics are still not in agreement over the attribution, vacillating between Botticelli and Filippino Lippi.

# HALL OF THE COLOSSUS

*The name of this room is not, as is usually believed, taken from Giambologna's plaster model, now placed at its centre, but from the model of one of Monte-cavallo's* Dioscuri, *displayed here in the last century. The panels on display follow on in chronological order from the route of the Florentine rooms and are therefore by painters working in the early decades of the 16th century. The room also temporarily houses some glass display cabinets with musical instruments, which will be definitively located in the rooms now being prepared in the new Luigi Cherubini State School of Music Museum.*

**GIAMBOLOGNA**
*Rape of the Sabine Women*

1582
Plaster cast
Height 410
Sculptures inv. no. 1071

This is the plaster model for the marble sculptured group which can be seen under the Loggia dei Lanzi in Piazza della Signoria. Giambologna's virtuosity here ventures to create for the first time a large-sized marble sculpture with a tightly-knit group of three figures, which almost form a single body, in a circular spiral movement seemingly without beginning or end. When the group was sculpted it did not have a definite subject but was presented by the artist as a simple exercise in skill; only later was it given the title *Rape of the Sabine Women*.

**ANDREA DEL SARTO**
*Christ as the Man
of Sorrows*

c. 1514-1520
Detached fresco
200×131
Inv. 1890 no. 8675

This fresco was re-moved in 1810 from the top of the staircase lead-ing to the novitiate in the Santissima Annun-ziata monastery in Flo-rence. Despite the poor condition of the work (perhaps also due to the detachment procedure which presented greater risks in that period than today) the figure of the suffering Christ, his pierced hands resting wearily on the stone of the tomb, still express-es the drama of death and pain with great in-tensity.

**MARIOTTO ALBERTINELLI**
*Annunciation*

1510
Oil on wood
335×230
Inv. 1890 no. 8643

This large panel decorated the chapel of the brotherhood of San Zanobi at the rectory of the Cathedral of Santa Maria del Fiore in Florence. After Albertinelli's death two other paintings were added to the sides depicting the *Removal of* *the body of San Zanobi* and *San Zanobi revives a boy* by Ridolfo del Ghirlandaio, with a stylistic majesty and essentiality perhaps never previously attained in his paintings.

**FRA BARTOLOMEO**
*The Prophets
Isaiah and Job*

c. 1514-1515

Oil on wood; 169×108
Inv. 1890 no. 1448 and 1449

These two recently restored panels came from the Billi Chapel in the basilica of the Santissima Annunziata in Florence. At their centre was the *Salvator Mundi and the Four Evangelists*, today on show in the Palatina Gallery. Cardinal Carlo de' Medici purchased the three pan-

IPSE ERIT SALVATOR MEVS

· IOB ·

els in 1631 and placed them in the Medici house in Piazza San Marco. In 1697 Prince Ferdinand took the central altarpiece to Palazzo Pitti as part of his personal collection, while the two *Prophets* were passed on to the Uffizi and then to the Accademia. The two *Prophets* were painted by Fra Bartolomeo immediately after his journey to Rome and are evidence of his meditations on Michelangelo's Sistine Chapel.

**PIETRO PERUGINO**
*Assumption*
*of the Virgin with*
*Saints John Gualberto,*
*Bernardo degli Uberti,*
*Benedict and Michael*

1500

Oil on wood; 415×246
Inv. 1890 no. 8366

This altarpiece was located on the high altar of the church in the Benedictine monastery of Vallombrosa.

Pietro Perugino painted it with a solid, expert technique using structures and drawings already tested on other, similar great compositions, and dwelling in his usual pleasant way on the decorative details like the Archangel Michael's sophisticated armour on the extreme right.

**FILIPPINO LIPPI
AND PIETRO PERUGINO**
*Deposition*
(and detail below)

1504 and 1507

Oil on wood
334×225
Inv. 1890 no. 8370

This painting was part of a grand wooden group commissioned by the friars of the Santissima Annunziata of Florence for their high altar. Filippino began work on it in 1504 and finished the upper part except for the body of Christ; he then died, and the work was completed in 1507 by Perugino who also painted the other panels to be inserted in the altar.

41

**GIOVANNI ANTONIO SOGLIANI**
*Dispute concerning the Immaculate Conception*

c. 1530
Oil on canvas
347×230
Inv. 1890 no. 3203

This panel shows the Doctors of the Church gathered around the body of Adam discussing the question of the Immaculate Conception of the Virgin Mary, a theme also depicted in Carlo Portelli's panel on the left side of the Tribuna beside the *David*. This work belongs to the specific historical period in which the Catholic Church was particularly intent on consolidating the Marian cult against diffusion of the Lutheran heresy.

# SIDE WINGS OF THE TRIBUNA

*Since the beginning of the 1980s this area has housed a series of works by artists who were contemporaries of Michelangelo, or slightly later. Among these are some of Alessandro Allori's large panels.*

**IACOPO PONTORMO**
*Venus and Cupid*
(and detail on the left)

c. 1535

Oil on wood
127×191
Inv. 1890 no. 1570

This painting was made from a cartoon drawn by Michelangelo, as can be seen from the sculptural forms of the Venus and the Cupid.

Venus' nudity was covered presumably only a short while after she was painted, because she appears already dressed in the copy by Vasari which can today be seen in the Palazzo Colonna in Rome. The painting was restored to its original condition by Ulisse Forni in 1852, revealing Pontormo's nude.

**ALESSANDRO ALLORI**
*Annunciation*

1578-1579
Oil on wood
445×285
Inv. 1890 no. 8662

This panel was commissioned by Sister Laura de' Pazzi for the convent of Montedomini, in whose church it was situated when the holy institution was suppressed and its furnishings confiscated by the State.

The severe and contained composition, suitable for a convent in a time of counter-reform, is softened by the charming still-life of the basket with clothes and the delicate flowers scattered on the floor.

**SANTI DI TITO**
*Christ's Deposition
from the Cross*

c. 1590
Oil on wood
200×168
Inv. 1890 no. 4637

The painting shows Christ removed from the cross surrounded by the Virgin Mary, Saint John the Baptist, Saint Catherine and a messenger wearing armour decorated with the insignia of the knights of St. Stephen. Despite various attempts by experts, the identity of this last figure has never been established with any certainty. The chromatic sensitivity of this painting tends to date the work at the beginning of the last decade of the century, the period in which Santi di Tito was most greatly influenced by Cigoli's emphasis on chromatic effects.

# Nineteenth Century Room

*The large Nineteenth Century Room was conceived and realised in order to provide the collection of plaster casts by Lorenzo Bartolini with a stable and definitive location. However the intention was also to offer the visitor tangible evidence of the 19th century academic origins of this Gallery, today mainly known for Michelangelo's* David.

**Lorenzo Bartolini,** *Monument to Nikolaj Demidov*

**LORENZO BARTOLINI**
*Monument
to Nikolaj Demidov*
(details)

Post 1828
Plaster
Sculptures inv.
nos. 1174-1177, 1209, 1221

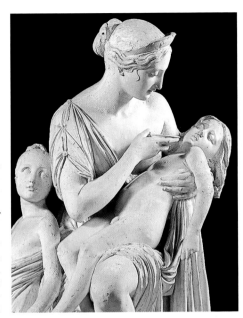

The commemorative monument to Count Nikolaj Demidov was commissioned by his sons Paul and Anatolij in 1828, on the death of their father.

Due however to various disruptions in the work, several times interrupted and restarted when the difficulties were overcome, it was only placed where it stands today (in Piazza Demidov, opposite Lungarno Serristori) in 1871. The work was finished by Romanelli, a pupil of Bartolini who took over his workshop. It was a grand and complex project, consisting of many statues, some larger than life, with complicated allegorical meaning. The plaster model of the central group, depicting the Count with his son Anatolij, has been lost.

# Byzantine Rooms

*The Florentine Gothic painting route starts in these rooms, which house many gold-leaf background panels in an absolutely unique collection of its kind. Displayed in the central room are works by artists predating Giotto or his contemporaries, like the Master of San Gaggio and Pacino di Buonaguida; in the right-hand room are Giotto's direct followers, Taddeo Gaddi, Bernardo Daddi, Iacopo del Casentino; in the left-hand room are the Orcagna family and their close collaborators.*

**MASTER OF THE MAGDALEN**
*Saint Mary Magdalene and Scenes from Her Life*

c.1280-1285

Tempera on wood; 164×76
Inv. 1890 no. 8466

This panel clearly exemplifies Florentine painting before Giotto, within whose circle this anonymous painter can be placed.

Giotto set up one of the most productive workshops in Florence between 1265 and 1290, and this painter also shows evidence of attention to the innovations introduced by Cimabue. In this sense, the small side scenes, which offer a direct and lively narrative of moments from the saint's life, are more attractive than the solemn central figure. A conspicuous example are the naturalistic landscape elements in the background of the *Noli me tangere* (depicted in the second scene on the left).

**MASTER
OF SAINT CECILIA**
*Enthroned Madonna*

c. 1290-1300

Tempera on wood
185×97
Inv. 1890 no. 5917

This is a work of fundamental importance for the history of 14th century Florentine painting. It is attributed to an anonymous contemporary and collaborator of Giotto, whose hand is recognisable also in some parts of the frescoes with *Scenes from the Life of Saint Francis* in the upper basilica of Assisi.

**PACINO DI BUONAGUIDA**
*Tree of Life*
(and details on the right)

c.1305-1310

Tempera on wood
248×151
Inv. 1890 no. 8459

With its vivid colours and sophisticated drawing (Pacino was also a famous illuminator), this painting mainly illustrates the content of Saint Bonaventure's *Lignum Vitae*, although there are also many scenes and scrolls alluding to biblical texts. In its entirety it appears as a large doctrinal page for meditation as well as an image to be admired. The subject of the illustration is the genealogy of Christ, who is shown nailed to the tree-shaped cross with its roots on a rocky mountain, symbolising Mt. Calvary.

**TADDEO GADDI**
*Scenes from
the life of Christ
and of Saint Francis*

(below: *Crucifixion,
Adoration of the Magi,
Stigmata of Saint
Francis, Saint Francis
upholds the church*)

c. 1333

Tempera on wood
41×29/36 (panels),
72×158 (lunettes)
Inv. 1890 nos. 8581-8603

These panels came from the sacristy of the basilica of Santa Croce where they decorated wooden furniture, perhaps a reliquary cupboard. The single episodes from the life of Saint Francis are illustrated in a parallel with the life of Christ: for example, the episode with the imposition of the stigmata corresponds to the Crucifixion. Taddeo Gaddi, Giotto's most direct pupil, was the first to include his master's innovations: note the solid volumetric disposition of the figures and the well-constructed architectural perspective, which indicate a *modus operandi* very far removed from the transcendent and ethereal world of Byzantine painting.

**BERNARDO DADDI**
*Painted Cross*

c. 1348
Tempera on wood
350×275
Inv. 1890 no. 442

This large, shaped crucifix possibly comes from the church of San Donato in Polverosa and was presumably placed above the high altar, hanging from the ceiling. In medieval churches this type of image was often placed on top of the iconostasis, i.e. the dividing wall between the presbytery and the choir, as is clearly shown in the Greccio nativity scene painted by Giotto in the basilica of St. Francis in Assisi.

**BERNARDO DADDI**
*Saint Lawrence
and Saint Bartholomew*

c. 1340

Tempera on wood
109×40 (each panel)
Inv. 1890
nos. 8706 and 8707

These two saints were part of a polyptych made for the chapel of Saint Bartholomew and Saint Lawrence in the church of the Carmine in Florence; at the polyptych's centre was a *Madonna with Child* and at the sides two or perhaps four *Saints*. The polyptych also probably had a predella.

These paintings reached us in an exceptionally integral state of preservation and allow us to fully appreciate the quality of Bernardo Daddi's work in around 1340, at the peak of his career.

### IACOPO DEL CASENTINO
*Saint Bartholomew*

c.1340
Tempera on wood
266×122
Inv. 1890 no. 440

This panel was commissioned straight after 1339 by the Grocers' Guild, who at that very time had erected their shrine on one of the pillars of the church of Orsanmichele and dedicated it to their patron, Saint Bartholomew. The pillars of the whole church of Orsanmichele were decorated during the 14th century with images of the patron saints of the various Guilds: this is because it was the delegated area for trade and its upper floor was actually used as a granary while the market was held in the loggia on the ground floor. The saint's face has been considerably damaged by cleaning with soda, presumably in the last century but fortunately the inexpert restorer must have realised the harm he was doing and refrained from continuing, as the rest of the panel is well-preserved.

**ANDREA ORCAGNA**
*Pentecost*
(whole and detail)

c. 1365
Tempera on wood
195×287
Deposits inv. no. 165

This triptych reveals the characteristics of Andrea's painting style in the last phase of his life; with its square spaces, the rigid frontal arrangement of the figures and the limited chromatic range, it must have fitted harmoniously in the Romanesque church of the Santi Apostoli in Florence, where it came from. In the second half of the 18th century it was transferred to the church of Badia, from where it was passed to the Accademia Gallery in 1939. It is likely that Andrea's younger brother Iacopo assisted in the painting work, and his hand can be seen in areas of softer, more blended application of colour in some of the apostles, and hints of softness in the volumetric construction.

**NARDO DI CIONE**
*Trinity*

1365
Tempera on wood
300×210
Inv. 1890 no. 8464

This impressive polyptych was commissioned by Giovanni Ghiberti for his chapel in the Chapter of Santa Maria degli Angeli. It was removed from there in about 1750 and taken to the Della Stufa Chapel, dedicated to Saint Andrew, and on this occasion Saint John was repainted to resemble Saint Andrew. Today the triptych has resumed its original appearance.

**IACOPO DI CIONE**
*Stories from
the Childhood of Christ*

c.1370
Tempera on wood
141×101
Inv. 1890 no. 5887

This panel was in the past attributed to an anonymous master known as the Master of Christ's Childhood because of the scenes depicted here, but has now been included in the early works of Iacopo di Cione, brother of Andrea Orcagna and quite close in his lively narrative style to Niccolò di Tommaso.

**MASTER OF THE RINUCCINI CHAPEL**
*Saint Bernard's vision*

1365-1370
Tempera on wood
175×200
Inv. 1890 no. 8463

The panel is the work of a painter who has remained anonymous, and who worked with Giovanni da Milano on the fresco decorations of the Rinuccini Chapel in Santa Croce, completing them when da Milano left Florence. Stylistically it is clearly the work of a painter trained in the Orcagna studio, with its strong sense of volumetric disposition and monumentality.

However, contact with the great Lombardian master has influenced his chromatic range making it warmer and brighter compared to the more adherent followers of Orcagna.

**IACOPO DI CIONE**
*Coronation
of the Virgin with
Saints and Prophets*

c. 1370
Tempera on wood
350×190
Inv. 1890 no. 456

This large panel was commissioned by the officials of the Mint, where the gold coin of Florence was struck (the florin). Gold, in fact, plays an important role in this luminous composition in which the throne disappears behind decorated tapestry drapery with naturalistic and geometric elements, sophisticated enough to be worthy of the most flamboyant Gothicism.

# First Floor Rooms

*These recently restored and rearranged rooms bring together the varied and exhaustive range of late Gothic Florentine painting.*
*These include portable altarpieces and grand polyptychs, as well as a collection of nine works by Lorenzo Monaco, an incomparably beautiful group of exceptional rarity, through which we can become familiar with the work of this great Gothic painter in all the phases of his artistic career.*

**GIOVANNI DA MILANO**
*Christ as the Man of Sorrows*

1365
Tempera on wood; 122×58
Inv. 1890 no. 8467

This small devotional panel represents one of the greatest achievements of 14th century painting in Florence after the death of Giotto. It was painted for the church of San Girolamo alla Costa, dated and signed, and at the bottom bears the coats of arms of the Strozzi and Rinieri families who obviously commissioned it. Giovanni da Milano's painting, with its intense sensitivity to colour and moving sentimentality offers an alternative to the severe style of Orcagna, which had dominated the gloomy period following the Great Plague of 1348. With Giovanni's work, Florence opened up to the new insistence of the International Gothic trend.

**ANDREA DI BONAIUTO**
*Saint Agnes*
*and Saint Domitilla*

c. 1365

Tempera on wood
66×28
Inv. 1890 no. 3145

Andrea di Bonaiuto (also known as Andrea da Firenze), a Florentine painter who trained in the studio of Nardo di Cione, brother of Andrea Orcagna, is famous above all for having frescoed the Spagnuoli Chapel in the Santa Maria Novella monastery.

This small diptych is stylistically and therefore chronologically close to that work and demonstrates the painter's knowledge and assimilation of the work of Giovanni da Milano, who was present and working in Florence in those very years. The two female figures shown here particularly stand out for the courtly sophistication of their costly clothes and the intense use of chiaroscuro.

**DON SILVESTRO DE' GHERARDUCCI**
*Virgin of Humility*

c.1370-1375
Tempera on wood
164×89
Inv. 1890 no. 3161

Silvestro de' Gherarducci entered the monastery of Santa Maria degli Angioli in 1348 aged nine. He worked with Lorenzo Monaco as a painter and illuminator, never losing the characteristic rich and colourful decorative elements which denote his Sienese origins. The *Virgin of Humility*, which depicts the Virgin Mary sitting on the ground on a cushion, is a subject particularly dear to late Gothic tastes.

**GIOVANNI DEL BIONDO**
*Annunciation*
*with Saints*
(and details on the right)

c. 1380
Tempera on wood
406×377
Inv. 1890 no. 8606

This large and complex polyptych was situated on the altar of the Cavalcanti Chapel in Santa Maria Novella. It came to us in excellent condition, complete with almost all its accessories, and constitutes an example of the high technical quality of the work of 14th century Florentine workshops.

**MARIOTTO DI NARDO**
*Virgin and Child Enthroned with Angels and Four Saints*

c. 1390-1395

Tempera on wood
165×242 (central part),
42×267 (predella)
Inv. 1890
nos. 8612, 8613
3258, 3259, 3260

This polyptych records the mature phase of Mariotto di Nardo's work. Mariotto was quite an active artist in Florence between the 14th and 15th centuries, also for commissions of a certain importance.

His success was probably due to the Orcagnesque elements in his style, the excessive hardness of which was diluted with warmer colouring and more char-ming decorative elements.

The work by Mariotto reached us complete with all its elements, i.e. the predella showing *Scenes from the Life of the Virgin* and the large cuspidate panels with the *Annunciation* and the *Crucifixion*, and thus provides us with an idea of how ornate the altars of the most important Medieval churches must have been.

**NICCOLÒ
DI PIETRO GERINI**
*Christ as the Man
of Sorrows*
(on the left)

c. 1404-1408

Tempera on wood
351×158
Inv. 1890
nos. 5048, 5066, 5067

This panel is a typical example of the work of the Orcagna-trained painter Niccolò di Pietro Gerini and comes from the Disciplinary Company of the Pellegrino in Santa Maria Novella. The brethren of the company are depicted on the cusp kneeling in the foreground before Christ dressed as a pilgrim, and on the predella in the act of burying one of the members of their Company. All the brethren wear white cloaks and their heads are covered by hoods, in order not to be recognised while carrying out works of charity. At the centre Christ rises from the tomb, showing the wounds in his hands and side, before the cross, on which are hung the symbols of the Passion: nails, whips, the spear and the sponge.

**SPINELLO ARETINO**
*Saint Stephen*

c. 1400-1405

Tempera on wood
92×33
Inv. 1890 no. 6287

The saint is depicted holding in his right hand the banner of the Wool Guild, which was quite a powerful corporation in Florence and the same motif is repeated on the sides of the predella. This little tabernacle demonstrates the preciosity of Spinello's later style, and to a greater extent, the small Crucifixion in the cusp panel, where the drapery of the crouching figures flows with inimitable elegance.

**ROSSELLO
DI IACOPO FRANCHI**
*Coronation
of the Virgin*
(and details below)

1422
Tempera on wood
344×300
Inv. 1890 no. 8460

This grand and highly decorated polyptych is the work of Rossello di Iacopo Franchi, an artist who trained in the late Gothic period and continued to paint his sweet and rather mannered figures until the end of his life (1456), long after the advent in Florence of Masaccio and the rise of the early Renaissance.

**LORENZO MONACO**
*The Oration
in the Garden*

c. 1395

Tempera on wood
222×109
Inv. 1890 no. 438

This is one of the oldest panels by Lorenzo Monaco and was painted for the Florentine monastery of Santa Maria degli Angeli, where the artist lived. His deep knowledge of Giotto's painting, who must have been directly known to him, is evident from the style, learned in the Orcagna studio.

However, at the same time the fluid and extended flowing of the drapery places his work within the modern taste for International Gothicism.

**LORENZO MONACO**
*Virgin Enthroned*
*with Saints*

1410
Tempera on wood
274×259
Inv. 1890 no. 468

This polyptych formerly decorated the church of San Bartolomeo in Montoliveto near Florence and confirms Lorenzo Monaco's ability with chromatic and decorative effects, even in works of larger dimensions. Having now fully mastered his expressive medium, the great master emphasises here the outlines of the figures with impeccable fluidity and harmony while the chromatic range seems infused with the purest light. It must be remembered that Lorenzo Monaco was also an illuminator and his pen decorated with gold and bright colours many of the manuscripts made in the monastery of Santa Maria degli Angioli, where he lived as a Camaldolensian monk.

SCA·CATHARINA    SCS·ANTONIUS    AVE·GRATIA·PLENA    ECCE·ANCILLA·DOMINI    SCS·PROCULUS    SCS·PRANCISC

**LORENZO MONACO**
*Annunciation*
(and details on the right)

c. 1418
Tempera on wood
210×229
Inv. 1890 no. 8458

Painted for the Floren-
tine Badia, this *Annun-
ciation* represents the
peak of Lorenzo Mona-
co's work; in the period
in which Masaccio, who
began the artistic Re-
naissance, was begin-
ning to work, the me-
dieval world is brought
to life with brilliant success in this work.

## THE COLLECTION OF RUSSIAN ICONS

*The collection of Russian icons, put together by the Grand Dukes of Lorraine, is displayed in the niches of the right-hand wall. The quality of these pieces is rather discontinuous and only rarely of exceptional calibre; therefore it might be said that the group as a whole is more significant for research and knowledge of the Lorraine passion for collecting rather than for the history of Russian art.*

**RUSSIAN SCHOOL**
*Saint Catherine*

18th century
Tempera on wood
32×27
Inv. 1890 no. 5979

Catherine is portrayed with her usual attributes, i.e. the palm of martyrdom in her right hand and the hooked wheel on which she was tortured before her head was cut off. The image is decorated with a crown and a fine silver-gilt frame.

**RUSSIAN SCHOOL**
*Dormitio Virginis*

17th century

Tempera on wood
44×31
Inv. 1890 no. 6147

This small, finely made panel depicts Our Lady lying on her death-bed surrounded by the apostles, while in his arms Christ raises his moth-er's soul, portrayed as a baby, and prepares to lead it into heaven.

**GHERARDO STARNINA**
*Virgin and Child with Angels and Two Saints*

c. 1407-1410
Tempera on wood
96×51
Inv. 1890 no. 441

Gherardo Starnina, a Florentine painter who also worked in Spain where he came into contact with the most advanced trends of International Gothicism, today tends to be identified by critics as the so-called Master of the Lively Child, an outstanding figure in early 15th century painting in Florence. He was noted for his linear finesse and the decorative nature of his elegant forms, and is almost a profane alter ego of Lorenzo Monaco.

**MASTER OF THE STRAUS MADONNA**
*Annunciation*
(and details on the right)

c. 1395-1405
190×200
Inv. 1890 no. 3146

This work came from the leper hospital of Sant'Eusebio al Prato and is attributed to a painter who was active between the end of the 14th century and the beginning of the 15th.

His identity is not known and he is usually known as the Master of the Straus Madonna from a *Madonna with Child* formerly in the Straus collection.

This is a painter of a very high standard, gifted with fine sensitivity to colour and who also pays attention to the volumetric structure of bodies and the perspective depth of the space.

**GIOVANNI TOSCANI**
*The Incredulity
of Saint Thomas*
(and details on the right)

c. 1420
Tempera on wood
240×112
Inv. 1890 no. 457

Giovanni Toscani was for a long time known as the Master of the *Griggs Crucifixion*, before his identity was discovered in 1966. The subject matter of this panel is commented on the dado at the bottom with the words "Touch that which is real like me and you will believe in justice combined in three people, which always exalts those who act justly". The sentence refers to a place where justice was administered, perhaps the court of Mercatanzia, around which he worked in 1419-1420; this date is in keeping with the Gothic characteristics of the work.

**BICCI
DI LORENZO**
*Saint Lawrence*

c. 1428
Tempera on wood
236×84
Inv. 1890 no. 471

This panel comes from
the laical company de-
voted to Saint Peter at
the church of San Pietro
a Monticelli. The saint
is shown standing on
the symbol of his mar-
tyrdom, the grille, while
in his left hand he holds
the palm and in the right
a red banner with a gold
star, perhaps the insignia
of the Company who
commissioned the work.
In the predella, in the
right-hand scene, Saint
Lawrence is depicted
freeing souls from Pur-
gatory, according to the
legend which claims
that as he died on Good
Friday, he was permit-
ted every Friday to re-
peat Christ's descent to
the underworld. The
scene on the left shows
the martyrdom inflict-
ed on him by his perse-
cutors. Bicci di Loren-
zo painted this work in
collaboration with Ste-
fano d'Antonio with
whom he "kept compa-
ny" (or as we would say
today "was in partner-
ship") from 1426 to 1434.

# INDEX

**ALBERTINELLI, MARIOTTO**
(Florence 1474-1515)
*Annunciation* 37

**ALLORI, ALESSANDRO**
(Florence 1535-1607)
*Annunciation* 44

**ANDREA DEL SARTO**
Andrea d'Agnolo, known as
(Florence 1486-1530)
*Christ as the Man of Sorrows* 36

**ANDREA DI BONAIUTO**
(Florence, documented from 1343-1377)
*Saint Agnes and Saint Domitilla* 62

**ANDREA DI GIUSTO**
Andrea Manzini, known as
(Florence, 1st half of 15th century)
*Madonna of the girdle* 26

**BARTOLINI, LORENZO**
(Savignano di Prato 1777-Florence 1850)
*Monument to Nikolaj Demidov* **46-47**

**BICCI DI LORENZO**
(Florence 1373-1452)
*Saint Lawrence* 77

**BOTTICELLI, SANDRO,**
Alessandro Filipepi, known as
(Florence 1445-1510)
*Virgin and Child with the Young
Saint John and Two Angels* 33

**BOTTICELLI, SANDRO** (?)
*Virgin of the Sea* 34

**BUONARROTI, MICHELANGELO**
(Caprese 1475-Rome 1564)
*David* 4, 8, 21-25
*Slaves: Atlas* 13, 19
*Slaves: the Awakening Slave* 16-17
*Slaves: the Bearded Slave* 16, 18
*Slaves: the Young Slave* 14-15
*Saint Matthew* 20

**BUONARROTI, MICHELANGELO** (?)
*Pietà from Palestrina* 8

**DADDI, BERNARDO**
(Florence c. 1290-1348)
*Painted crucifix* 55
*St. Lawrence and St. Bartholomew* 54

**FRA BARTOLOMEO**
Bartolomeo di Paolo del Fattorino, known as
(Savignano di Prato 1472-Florence 1517)
*The Prophet Isaiah
and the Prophet Job* 38-39

**GADDI, TADDEO**
(Florence, documented from 1327 to 1366)
*Scenes from the Life of Christ
and of Saint Francis* 52

**GERINI, NICCOLÒ DI PIETRO**
(Florence, documented from 1368 to 1415)
*Christ as the Man of Sorrows* 67

**GHIRLANDAIO**
Domenico Bigordi, known as IL
(Florence 1449-1494)
*Saint Stephen
between Saints James and Peter* 32

**GIAMBOLOGNA**
Jean de Boulogne, known as
(Douai 1529-Florence 1608)
*Rape of the Sabine Women* 35

**GIOVANNI DA MILANO**
(documented from 1346 to 1369)
*Christ as the Man of Sorrows* 61

**GIOVANNI DEL BIONDO**
(Florence, documented from 1356 to 1399)
*Annunciation* 64

**IACOPO DEL CASENTINO**
Iacopo Landini known as
(Florence 1297-c. 1358)
*Saint Bartholomew* 55

**IACOPO DI CIONE**
(Florence, documented from 1365 to 1398)
*Coronation of the Virgin* 60
*Stories from the Childhood of Christ* 58

**LIPPI, FILIPPINO**
(Prato 1457-Florence 1504)
*Deposition* 41

**LORENZO MONACO**
Pietro di Giovanni, known as
(Siena? c. 1370-Florence c. 1423)
*Annunciation* 71
*Virgin Enthroned with Saints* 70
*Oration in the Garden* 69

LO SCHEGGIA
Giovanni di Ser Giovanni, known as
(San Giovanni Valdarno 1406-
Florence 1486)
*"Cassone Adimari"* 28-29

MASTER OF THE RINUCCINI CHAPEL
(Florence , documented from 1350 to c. 1380)
*Saint Bernard's Vision* 59
MASTER OF THE MAGDALEN
(Florence, 2nd half of 13th century)
*Saint Mary Magdalene
and Scenes from Her Life* 48
MASTER OF THE STRAUS MADONNA
(Florence, active between end
of 14th century and beginning of 15th)
*Annunciation* 75
MASTER OF THE SAINT CECILIA
(Florence 1290-c. 1330)
*Enthroned Madonna* 49
MARIOTTO DI NARDO
(Florence, documented from 1394 to 1424)
*Virgin and Child Enthroned
with Angels and Four Saints* 65

NARDO DI CIONE
(Florence, documented from c. 1343 to 1366)
*Trinity* 57
NERI DI BICCI
(Florence 1419-1492)
*Annunciation* 31

ORCAGNA,
Andrea di Cione, known as L'
(Florence, documented from 1343 al 1368)
*Pentecost* 56

PACINO DI BUONAGUIDA
(Florence, documented from 1303 to 1339)
*Tree of Life* 50-51
PAOLO UCCELLO
Paolo di Dono, known as
(Pratovecchio 1397-Florence 1475)
*Scenes of Hermit Life* 27
PERUGINO
Pietro Vannucci, known as IL

(Città della Pieve c. 1448-Fontignano 1523)
*Assumption of the Virgin* 40
*Deposition* 41
PONTORMO
Jacopo Carrucci,
known as IL
(Pontorme, Empoli 1494-Florence 1556)
*Venus and Cupid* 43

ROSSELLI, COSIMO
(Florence 1439-1507)
*Saint Barbara* 30
ROSSELLO DI IACOPO FRANCHI
(Florence 1377-1456)
*Coronation of the Virgin* 68
RUSSIAN SCHOOL
*Saint Catherine* 72
*Dormitio Virginis* 73

SANTI DI TITO
(Sansepolcro 1536-Florence 1603)
*Deposed Christ* 45
SILVESTRO DE' GHERARDUCCI, DON
(Florence 1339-1399)
*Virgin of Humility* 63
SOGLIANI, GIOVANNI ANTONIO
(Florence 1492-1544)
*Dispute concerning
the Immaculate Conception* 42
SPINELLO ARETINO
(Arezzo c. 1350-1411)
*Saint Stephen* 67
STARNINA, GHERARDO
(Florence 1354-c. 1413)
*Virgin and Child with Angels
and Two Saints* 74

TOSCANI, GIOVANNI
(Florence, c. 1370-1430)
*Incredulity of Saint Thomas* 76

Printed in July 1999
by Giunti Industrie Grafiche S.p.A. – Prato – Italy